Soft Skills Sleuths

ATTITUDE

T0027036

INVESTIGATING LIFE SKILLS SUCCESS

Diane Lindsey Reeves with Connie Hansen
Illustrations by Ruth Bennett

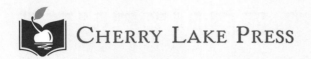

CHERRY LAKE PRESS

Published in the United States of America by Cherry Lake Publishing Group
Ann Arbor, Michigan
www.cherrylakepublishing.com

Created and produced by Bright Futures Press
www.brightfuturespress.com

Reading Advisor: Marla Conn, MS, Ed., Literacy specialist, Read-Ability, Inc.
Illustrator: Ruth Bennett
Cover and Page Designer: Kathy Heming
Design Elements: © mijatmijatovic/Shutterstock.com; © GoodStudio/Shutterstock.com;
    © Denis Cristo/Shutterstock.com; © Lorelyn Medina/Shutterstock.com; © Yaroshenko Olena/
    Shutterstock.com; © rangsan paidaen/Shutterstock.com

Cherry Lake Press is an imprint of Cherry Lake Publishing Group.

Library of Congress Cataloging-in-Publication Data has been filed and is available at catalog.loc.gov

Cherry Lake Publishing Group would like to acknowledge the work of the Partnership for 21st Century
Learning, a Network of Battelle for Kids. Please visit http://www.battelleforkids.org/networks/p21
for more information.

Printed in the United States of America
Corporate Graphics

TABLE OF CONTENTS

What Are Soft Skills and

Skills are needed to succeed at any job you can imagine. Different jobs require different skills. Professional baseball players need good batting and catching skills. Brain surgeons need steady hands and lots of practice with a scalpel. These are examples of **hard skills** necessary to do specific jobs.

Everyone needs "**soft skills**" to succeed in life. Soft skills get personal. They are about how you behave and treat people. Soft skills are the skills you need to be the very best *you* at home, work, and school.

"Sounds good," you say. "But I don't have a job. Why do I need to worry about soft skills?"

Ahh, but you do have a job. In fact, you have a very important job. You are a student, and your job is to learn as much as you can. Learning soft skills makes you a better student now. It also gets you ready to succeed in any career you choose later.

Attitude is a way of feeling or acting toward a person, thing, or situation. Your attitude is expressed not only in the things you say and do. It also shows in the *way* you say and do things. Your attitude shows, and it affects the people around you. Having a good attitude is a choice you make every day.

In this book, you get to be a soft skills **sleuth**. You will track down clues about what having a good (and not so good!) attitude looks like. You will **investigate** four soft skill qualities having to do with attitude:

- **Courteous**
- **Positive**
- **Confident**
- **Responsible**

Why Do I Need Them?

HOW TO USE THIS BOOK

Here's how you can be a soft skills sleuth. In each chapter:

 Gather the facts. Read the description about the soft skill.

 Read the case file. Check out a situation where soft skills are needed.

 Investigate the case. Look for clues showing soft skills *successes* and soft skills *mistakes*. Keep track of the clues on a blank sheet of paper.

 Crack the case. Did you spot all the clues?

SOFT SKILL #1 · · · · · ·

Courtesy and kindness go hand in hand. If you do something kind, it is also **courteous**. If you do something courteous, it is also kind. It's two good things for the price of one!

Every day you will find lots of ways to be courteous. It starts with the morning rush at home. Everyone is dashing around, trying to get out the door. How can you show a courteous attitude? Maybe it's helping your sister find her shoes. Maybe it's surprising your parent by packing *their* lunch for a change.

Courtesy doesn't stop at home. Take it with you wherever you go. It is always welcome on the school bus, in your classroom, and at all the activities that make up your day. A courteous attitude puts other people first. It is the opposite of a rude, selfish attitude.

Courtesy means going out of your way to make the day better for someone else. It doesn't matter how big or small your action is. Once you pick up the courtesy habit, you will find many opportunities to practice **random** acts of kindness that perk up your day-to-day life. Courtesy is an attitude booster. It lifts the spirits of everyone it touches.

Random Acts of Kindness

- Sit next to the new kid at lunch.
- Pick up litter around your school.
- Write a thank-you note to your teacher.
- Set the table for dinner without being asked.
- Offer to help rake your neighbor's leaves or shovel their sidewalk.
- Spend time with your grandparents.

"No act of kindness, no matter how small, is ever wasted."
—Aesop

COURTEOUS

SOFT SKILLS CASE #1: COURTEOUS

It's the school dance. It's an exciting and nerve-racking experience for all! A little courtesy goes a long way in making this fun for everyone. Can you spot acts of kindness that are putting the students at ease? **Is anyone making it harder for others to enjoy themselves?** Dance on over to the next page and let your investigation begin.

DO:
Investigate courteous successes and mistakes!

DO NOT:
Write in this book!

THEY COULD HAVE DANCED ALL NIGHT

COURTEOUS

Common courtesy is a good thing to bring to school dances. How is it on display at this one?

Did you **find** all the successes and **MISTAKES**?

Start here!

Mistake.
Standing around and gossiping about the other kids.

Success!
Letting someone go before you.

Mistake.
Someone forgot to dress for success.

Mistake.
Standing around and missing out on the fun.

··▶ CASE NOTES

Courtesy and kindness go hand-in-hand!

Success!
Let's dance!

Did you find them all?

Mistake.
How about taking turns with the dance partner, girls?

Success!
Hello, friend, I'd like you to meet . . .

Success!
Sharing the fun with a friend.

Mistake.
Hogging the dance floor with way-too-big moves.

SOFT SKILL #2

People think about and see the world in two very different ways. Some have a **positive** attitude, which makes them **optimistic** and open to opportunities. They look on the bright side of life. They think in terms of "I can" and "It is possible." A positive attitude is upbeat and encouraging.

Other people see things in a more negative way. The opposite of an optimistic attitude is a **pessimistic** one. People who think this way say things like "I can't" and "Things will never work out." It sees the worst in things and drags you and those around you down. But remember being pessimistic is different from depression. If you feel depressed, reach out to a parent or teacher for help.

Thinking about all the ways that something can go wrong is a gloomy mind-set. A positive mind-set considers how many ways things can go right! You can shift your focus to change a negative attitude into a positive one.

It starts with the way you talk to yourself. It is hard to be positive if your mind is busy **criticizing** yourself. The first step toward a positive attitude is to shut down the inner critic. When your mind says "I can't do this," tell it "I can give it my best shot." When it says "I'll never learn this stuff," tell it "Take it one step at a time." Treat yourself like you'd treat your very best friend.

A positive mind-set gives you more confidence, improves your mood, and reduces stress. Do yourself a favor and think positive!

Pardon Me, but Your Attitude Is Showing!

- Crack more jokes.
- Exercise your bad moods away.
- Stop negative thoughts in their tracks.
- Name three things you are thankful for.
- Think about the best parts of your day before you go to sleep.

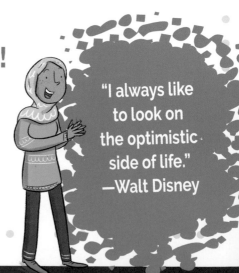

"I always like to look on the optimistic side of life."
—Walt Disney

⏵ POSITIVE

SOFT SKILLS CASE #2: POSITIVE

Older students can help younger ones learn to read by becoming reading buddies. The younger kids learn to be better readers. The older kids learn to be better leaders. It's a win-win for everyone. Ms. Leafgren's class of second graders looks forward to reading with their reading buddies every week.

It works best when everyone brings a positive attitude. **How is this session of reading buddies working out?** Turn the page to find out.

DO:
Investigate positive successes and mistakes!

DO NOT:
Write in this book!

A POSITIVE ATTITUDE IS CONTAGIOUS

POSITIVE

Read between the lines and find which reading buddies have positive attitudes. Which ones are putting out a negative vibe?

Start here!

Mistake.
How about sharing some of those books?

Mistake.
Acting too bored to care.

Success!
Paying attention says thanks for the help.

Mistake.
Making fun of your reading buddy.

Did you **find** all the successes and **MISTAKES**?

··▶ CASE NOTES

Does your attitude set a good example?

Success!
Let's read it again!

Did you find them all?

Mistake.
Nanny, nanny, boo boo. Catch me if you can!

Success!
Taking good care of the books.

Success!
Your turn to tell me a story, little buddy.

SOFT SKILL #3

Remember the story of "Goldilocks and the Three Bears"? Everything those bears encountered was either too much, too little, or just right. Confidence is a little like that story. Being too **confident** says "I can do everything because I am so great." It involves a lot of bragging. Too little confidence says "I'm too scared to try anything new." As a result, new opportunities are missed. Confidence that is just right says "I can do this" and you do it.

Being confident means trusting and having faith in your abilities. The good news is that confidence is a skill you can learn. That's because it comes from experience. The saying "Practice makes perfect" is true. You set out to learn a new skill. You practice it until you finally master it. Then—presto—you build your confidence!

Being confident about one thing gives you the courage to try something else. That's how confidence grows. You learn that you are a capable person, and that gives you confidence to face all kinds of situations. Keep it going and you'll learn all kinds of new things.

Become More Confident By . . .

- Looking your best when you go out.
- Smiling, standing tall, and looking people in the eye.
- Getting to know yourself better.
- Setting small goals and achieving them.
- Keeping a positive attitude.
- Giving yourself a break and learning from your mistakes.
- Knowing that everything doesn't have to be perfect.

"Good manners are just a way of showing other people that we have respect for them."
—Bill Kelly

CONFIDENT

SOFT SKILLS CASE #3: CONFIDENT

Skateboarding is an exciting after-school activity. It's lots of fun if you know what you are doing. But it takes skill to learn those cool high-speed tricks. Confidence comes with lots of practice. Practice builds skills and abilities so you can enjoy this challenging sport.

Take a look at the skatepark scene on the next page. Some of the students have good reason to be confident of their skateboarding abilities. Others are clearly amateurs. **There are some who are a bit overconfident and need to bail before they get hurt.** Which ones are which?

DO:
Investigate confident successes and mistakes!

DO NOT:
Write in this book!

CONFIDENT

Confident people know when to go for it.
They also know when it is time to back off.
Who is making confident choices here?

Did you **find** all the successes and **MISTAKES**?

Start here!

Mistake.
Um, do you really
think the blindfold
is a good idea?

Success!
Taking the time to
try a new trick.

Mistake.
Making fun of the
other skaters.

Success!
Making the rounds
like a champ.

Remember that you get good at what you practice.

Mistake.
Being too scared to try.

Success!
Showing a friend how it's done.

Did you find them all?

Success!
You can do it! Pep talks encourage others to try new things.

Mistake.
Standing in the way of someone else's success.

Mistake.
Sitting on the board is for amateurs.

SOFT SKILL #4

Responsible people are trustworthy. They are dependable and reliable. They are sensible and mature. They think things through carefully and make good decisions. Are you getting a sense of why this soft skill is so important to learn? All of these things say good things about a person.

Being responsible means doing what you are supposed to do, when you are supposed to do it. It isn't always easy. Like other attitudes, being responsible is a choice. But it is always the right choice to make.

Your first job as a responsible human is to learn to take care of yourself. That means getting your homework in on time and helping with the dinner dishes without being asked. It means eating healthy foods and getting enough rest. Right now your parents, teachers and other adults remind you to do these things. Taking more responsibility for yourself has an upside. It comes with new freedoms and privileges!

Being responsible keeps you out of trouble. It also makes it easier for people to like and trust you. This is important now as a student and as part of a family. It will get even more important as you get older, start your career, and build an adult life.

Responsible
People . . .

- Earn other people's trust.
- Say what they mean and mean what they say.
- Take care of themselves and others.
- Admit their mistakes and make things right.
- Try not to complain and avoid making excuses.
- Show up on time.

"The man who complains about the way the ball bounces is likely the one who dropped it."
—Lou Holtz

RESPONSIBLE

SOFT SKILLS CASE #4: RESPONSIBLE

Ms. Bailey's class is doing a community service project at the animal shelter. There are dogs that need walking. Some need a bath. The cats need to be fed. Some want to be cuddled. And someone's got to help with scooping the, um, you know what . . .

Are Ms. Bailey's students up to the task? Turn the page and check out the responsible choices they are making.

DO:
Investigate responsible successes and mistakes!

DO NOT:
Write in this book!

RESPONSIBILITY GOES TO THE DOGS (AND CATS)!

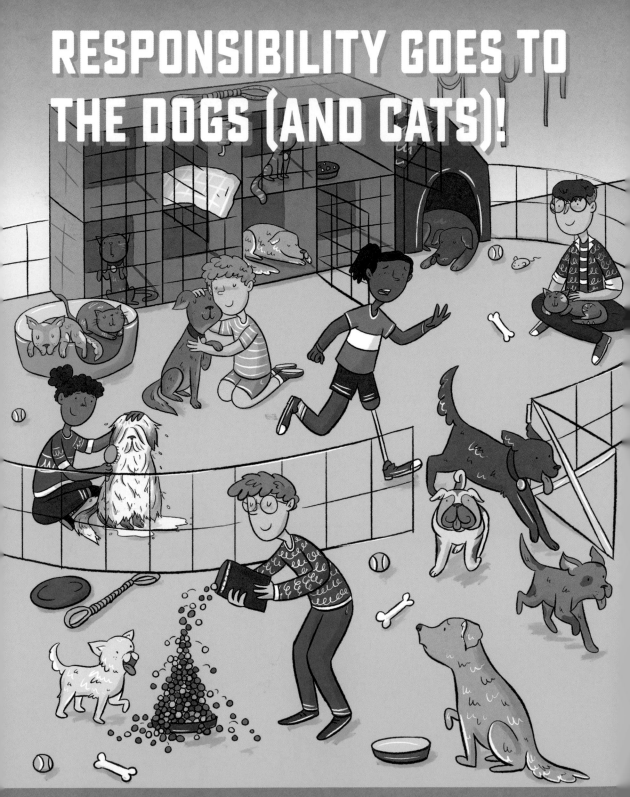

RESPONSIBLE

Which of these students would you trust to care for a beloved pet? Who needs to work a little harder to be responsible?

Did you find all the successes and MISTAKES?

Start here!

Success!
Walking pets when they need it.

Success!
Feeding the pet what they need to stay healthy.

Mistake.
Yelling at the pets instead of training them.

Mistake.
Letting someone else do the dirty work.

CASE NOTES

Can You Count On *You* to Make Responsible Choices?

Success!
It's chow time!

Mistake.
Who let the dawgs out?

Did you find them all?

Mistake.
Sharing too much of a good thing at feeding time.

Mistake.
Meow. How about brushing the cats' hair too?

Success!
Showing the pets some love.

WHAT HAVE YOU Learned?

......→ ATTITUDE QUIZ

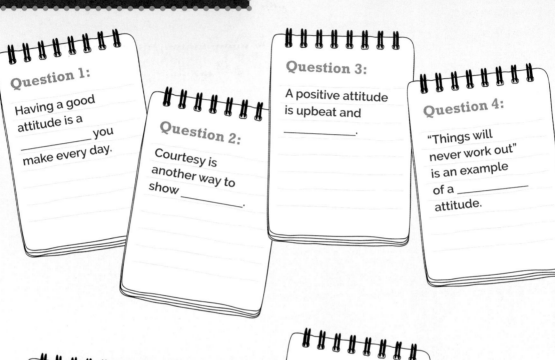

Question 1:
Having a good attitude is a _____ you make every day.

Question 2:
Courtesy is another way to show _____.

Question 3:
A positive attitude is upbeat and _____.

Question 4:
"Things will never work out" is an example of a _____ attitude.

Question 5:
To have _____ means that you trust yourself.

Question 6:
It takes _____ to be confident in a new skill.

Question 7:
The first person you need to take responsibility for is _____.

Question 8:
Responsibility builds _____ with other people.

Attitude
soft skills
start here!

GLOSSARY

attitude (AT-ih-tood) opinions and feelings about someone or something that affect how a person behaves

confident (KAHN-fih-duhnt) self-assured; having a strong belief in your own abilities

courteous (KUR-tee-uhs) polite, respectful, and considerate

criticizing (KRI-tuh-sai-zuhng) finding fault, disapproving

hard skills (HAHRD SKILZ) specific skills needed to do a specific job

investigate (in-VES-tih-gate) to gather information or clues about something

optimistic (ahp-tuh-MIS-tik) believing that things will usually turn out well or for the best

pessimistic (pes-uh-MIS-tik) always seeing the worst side of a situation or believing the worst will happen

positive (PAH-zih-tiv) helpful or constructive; upbeat and optimistic

random (RAN-duhm) without any order or purpose

responsible (rih-SPAHN-suh-buhl) assuming the duty to do something; trustworthy

sleuth (SLOOTH) a detective, or person who is good at finding facts and clues

soft skills (SAWFT SKILZ) behaviors and personality traits people use every day to succeed in life

INDEX

ABOUT THE AUTHORS ◄ •

Diane Lindsey Reeves likes to write books that help students figure out what they want to be when they grow up. She mostly lives in Washington, D.C., but spends as much time as she can in North Carolina and South Carolina with her grandkids.

Connie Hansen spent 25 years teaching college students about successful life skills. She lives in Lynchburg, Virginia where her favorite thing to do is play with her grandchildren. Her happy place is the beach!

• • • • • • • • • • • • • • • ► ABOUT THE ILLUSTRATOR

Ruth Bennett lives in a small country village in the heart of Norfolk, England, with her two cats, Queen Elizabeth and Queen Victoria. She loves petting dogs, watching movies, and drawing, of course!